TONY CRAGG AT GOODWOOD

FOREWORD BY WILFRED AND JEANNETTE CASS

We founded the Cass Sculpture Foundation at Goodwood, a registered charity, a decade ago, and could never have anticipated that we'd be celebrating our tenth anniversary with a unique exhibition of works from one of the world's leading sculptors, Tony Cragg. Despite being a recipient of the Turner Prize, member of the Royal Academy and the holder of numerous professorships around the world, Tony's work is probably less familiar in the UK than on the international arts stage.

His work is of such outstanding quality and vision that it was a natural choice for us to feature him on our new four-acre site called the Chalk Pit, which we created especially for our one-man exhibitions. Part of the Foundation's mission is to promote and advance the public's understanding of twenty-first century British sculpture, and this book is being published as part of its ongoing education programme.

But it is more that just a book presenting finished pieces of sculpture. Instead, it describes the whole process involved in creating the largest exhibition of Tony's outdoor sculptures in Britain to date. It shows the development of the exhibition from conception to the creation of the pieces in Tony's studios in Wuppertal, Germany, and through to the arrival and installation of the sculptures here at Goodwood.

It reveals both the process behind Tony's working practice and how the Cass Sculpture Foundation created one of the most ambitious sculpture projects ever realised in collaboration with a British artist. Photographer Leon Chew was commissioned to record the exhibition's development, providing a valuable pictorial record. I hope that you will also enjoy Dr Jon Wood's essay and Jane Duncan's article on this exhibition and Tony's works.

Our heartfelt thanks go to our great friend Tony, who has supported the Cass Sculpture Foundation from its very beginning.

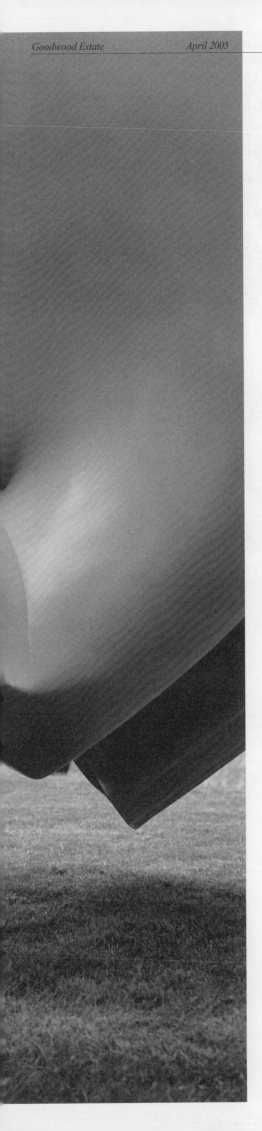

Declination

Materials/
Bronze
Dimensions/
2.4 x 2.3 x 3.6m
Weight/
2.7 tonnes

Declination

Materials/
Bronze
Dimensions/
2.4 x 2.3 x 3.6m
Weight/
2.7 tonnes

Declination

Materials/
Bronze
Dimensions/
2.4 x 2.3 x 3.6m
Weight/
2.7 tonnes

Declination

Materials/
Bronze
Dimensions/
2.4 x 2.3 x 3.6m
Weight/
2.7 tonnes

Declination

Materials/
Bronze
Dimensions/
2.4 x 2.3 x 3.6m
Weight/
2.7 tonnes

Tongue in Cheek
Materials/
Bronze
Dimensions/
1.3 x 1.7 x 2.3m
Weight/
0.8 tonnes

Tongue in Cheek
Materials/
Bronze
Dimensions/
1.3 x 1.7 x 2.3m
Weight/
0.8 tonnes

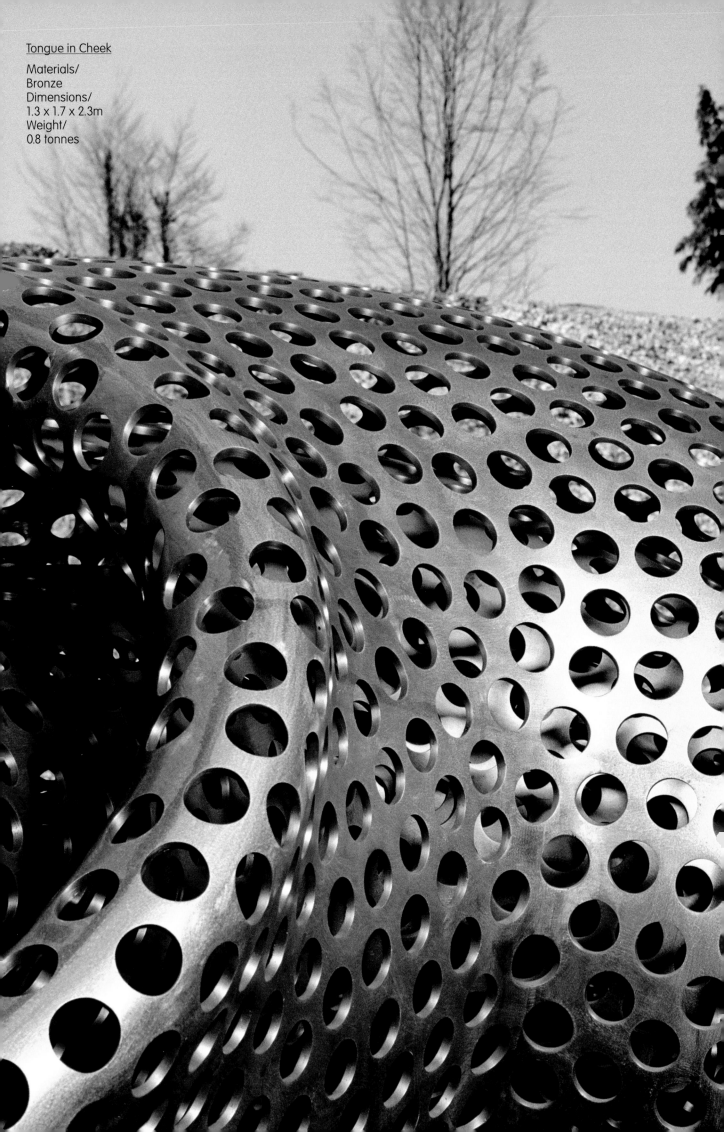

Tongue in Cheek
Materials/
Bronze
Dimensions/
1.3 x 1.7 x 2.3m
Weight/
0.8 tonnes

Bent of Mind

Materials/
Bronze
Dimensions/
4.7 x 2.7 x 2.7m
Weight/
5.5 tonnes

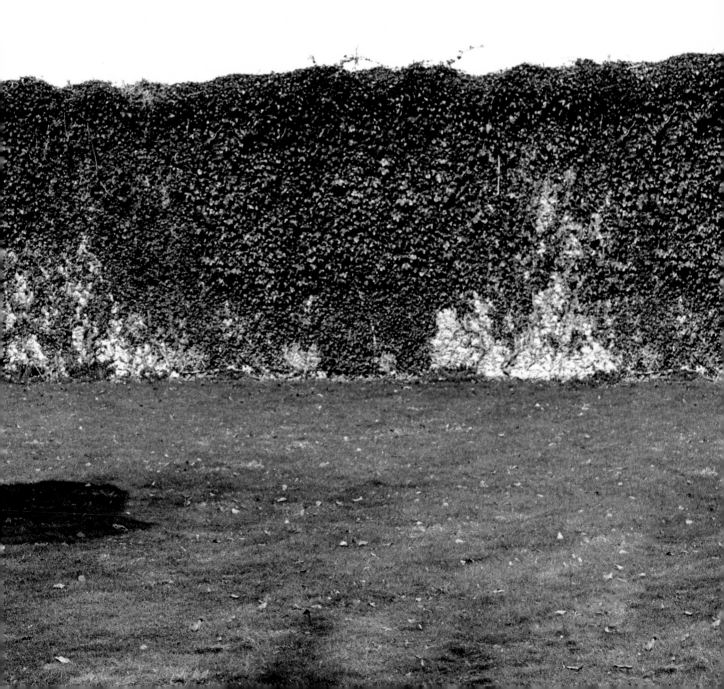

Bent of Mind

Materials/
Bronze
Dimensions/
4.7 x 2.7 x 2.7m
Weight/
5.5 tonnes

Bent of Mind

Materials/
Bronze
Dimensions/
4.7 x 2.7 x 2.7m
Weight/
5.5 tonnes

Here Today Gone Tomorrow

Materials/
Stone
Dimensions/
4.5 x 1.2 x 1.2cm (each)
Weight/
14 tonnes

Here Today Gone Tomorrow

Materials/
Stone
Dimensions/
4.5 x 1.2 x 1.2cm (each)
Weight/
14 tonnes

Sinbad

Materials/
Bronze
Dimensions/
1.6 x 3.1 x 1.7m
Weight/
2.7 tonnes

Sinbad

Materials/
Bronze
Dimensions/
1.6 x 3.1 x 1.7m
Weight/
2.7 tonnes

Formulations (Stance)

Materials/
Bronze
Dimensions/
2.2 x 1 x 1m
Weight/
0.6 tonnes

Formulations (Stance)

Materials/
Bronze
Dimensions/
2.2 x 1 x 1m
Weight/
0.6 tonnes

Ferryman

Materials/
Bronze
Dimensions/
3.9 x 1.9 x 1.2cm
Weight/
1.3 tonnes

Ferryman

Materials/
Bronze
Dimensions/
3.9 x 1.9 x 1.2cm
Weight/
1.3 tonnes

I'm Alive

Materials/
Stainless Steel
Dimensions/
2.5 x 3.9 x 3.6m
Weight/
4 tonnes

I'm Alive

Materials/
Stainless Steel
Dimensions/
2.5 x 3.9 x 3.6m
Weight/
4 tonnes

Point of View

Materials/
Stainless Steel
Dimensions/
3 x 0.8 x 0.7m
Weight/
0.3 tonnes

Bulb

Materials/
Stone
Dimensions/
3.3 x 1.8 x 1.8m
Weight/
15 tonnes

Bulb
Materials/
Stone
Dimensions/
3.3 x 1.8 x 1.8m
Weight/
15 tonnes

TONY
CRAGG
AT
GOODWOOD

ESSAY
ARTICLE
BIOGRAPHY
SCULPTURE-
INFORMATION
EXHIBITIONS

IN REMEMBRANCE OF THINGS FAST— THE SCULPTURE OF TONY CRAGG

BY DR JON WOOD, HENRY MOORE INSTITUTE

Tony Cragg once exhibited a meteorite. It was 'years ago', but also 'yesterday': twenty-eight years ago, to be precise, and Cragg was twenty-eight years old at the time. The year 1977 was very important for the sculptor: he graduated from the Royal College of Art and left London for Wuppertal, where he continues to live to this day. Alongside the comings and goings of that milestone year — which saw him showing at the Lisson Gallery and in the Silver Jubilee Outdoor Sculpture Show at Battersea Park — this small contribution to a group exhibition at the Fine Arts Building in New York has been somewhat overlooked. I would like to begin with this early work because it raises questions and hints at desires that, despite the continuing developments of Cragg's oeuvre, still energise his work today. Though very different, of course, in look, form, material and scale, it is also of particular relevance to his recent Early Forms and Rational Beings, of which some prime examples are included in this large outdoor exhibition staged by the Cass Sculpture Foundation at Goodwood.

Like the later Early Forms and Rational Beings, Meteorite plays out interesting tensions between speed and stasis, between the quick and the dead. Cragg at the time was endeavouring to locate his work and practice beyond the example of Minimalism, Land Art and Arte Povera, with a keen eye on the work of Joseph Beuys and Marcel Duchamp. Meteorite, shown on a shelf in the company of one of his crushed stone works and a constellation of silver stars, was a knowing riposte and potent proposition. Might this static object out-blast a serried row of firebricks, run rings around a stone circle, outwit a paperweight or a suspended rock, and outpace an erratic boulder? Beuys' use of the volcanic poetry of basalt was then still a few years off and, although Cragg's Meteorite was somewhat resonant of Duchamp's earlier found objects, it was appropriated from extraterrestrial, cosmic and galactic realms, as opposed to everyday, earthly life.[1] Despite the pull of these artistic co-ordinates, Meteorite was a foreign 'heavenly body', beautifully out of time, out of place and out of space.[2]

Similar observations could be made about I'm Alive. First made out of carbon and kevlar, the sculpture on display in the grounds of Goodwood is a version made in polished steel. It also looks 'out of this world' and 'just landed', and sits serpentine, twisting on the grass like a huge, extraterrestrial silverfish. Static, but restlessly reflective, it seduces us as viewers — sucking us up and stretching our imaginations along, around and into the surface, depth and movement of the sculpture. We are now also in the company of Brancusi, and as with his Fish, Cragg's sculpture is not a representation but a portrayal of an idea, an essence, a distillation, a movement. In terms of artistic trajectories we have moved, between these two works of Cragg's, from ballistics to balletics: where in 1977 we had a restless full stop, now we have an animated, quizzical speech mark or inverted comma.

Since Cragg works in open series and over a number of years, playing with and developing (rather like Brancusi) a range of solutions across 'family groups' of sculptures, the underlying concerns driving the work surface in different ways and manifest themselves at different stages. This gives the work collective and directional thrust, as well as a depth, range and togetherness, in which connections are to be seen at various levels and times, and between different materials, forms, objects and images. It also reveals an artistic creativity and a sculptural imagination that learns as it goes along, accumulating ideas and consolidating forms, from work to work, from group to group. There is a constant preoccupation with formal, as well as material, qualities — shape, volume, surface, skin, colour — but also with developing personal, intuitive, physical, intellectual and psychological relationships with them in the private studio, in the larger workshops, in the foundry and then beyond.

The paradoxical combination of speed and stasis within a single work, that classic sculptural challenge and conundrum, has been one of the most enduring concerns in Cragg's oeuvre. It has driven many of his 'signs of life' (a phrase

1/
See Joseph Beuys' *The End of the Twentieth Century* (1983–85), in the Tate's collection and, for example, the marble blocks caged inside Marcel Duchamp's *Why Not Sneeze, Rose Sélavy?* (1921), at the Philadelphia Museum of Art.

2/
Cragg has also referred to this work as 'a material in the house of space'. These quotations come from an interview with Tony Cragg, conducted by Jon Wood, for the Artists' Lives Project of the National Life Story Collection (National Sound Archive, British Library, London), June and December 2004. These quotations come from Tape 13/33.

3/
This phrase serves as the title of a comprehensive book of Cragg's work, *Tony Cragg: Signs of Life*, Richter Verlag, Düsseldorf, 2003.

4/
Cragg has always been an energetic and passionate spokesman for sculpture, as has often been noted. See, for example, Lewis Biggs, Tony Cragg: Energy in Dialogue, in *Tony Cragg: Holzkristall Woodcrystal*, Kunstverein & Stiftung, Springhornhof, 2000, pp.7–11.

5/
'Never at Rest' is also the title of one of Cragg's favourite books (Richard S. Westfall's *Never at Rest: A Biography of Isaac Newton*, Cambridge University Press, 1980).

6/
'Tony Cragg Interviewed by Lynne Cooke', in *Tony Cragg*, exh. Catalogue. Arts Council of Great Britain, London, 1987, pp. 36.

7/
Tony Cragg interview, NLSC, 2004, Tape 24/33.

8/
Ibid., Tape 21/33.

that is dear to him) and has taken shape in many materials and colours over the years.[3] It can be observed across numerous works, from the plastic wall relief <u>Self-Portrait</u> (1982), in which Cragg placed darts, bricks, bottles, arrows and knives, hurtling from above towards his silhouetted body, to the tornadic dynamism of the <u>Flotsam</u> sculptures (1997–2001). The fact that many of Cragg's works incorporate moments and passages of self-portraiture serves to remind of us of the urgency of this dynamic for the artist: how personally he is implicated in things and, in turn, how personally he wants us to take things. It is clearly a dynamic, one might say predicament even, that animates him, and that goes right to the very heart not only of his practice, but also of his sense of sculpture's history and his vision for its future.[4]

At the core of this dynamic is Cragg's constant, peripatetic exploration of the traditional idea of sculpture as a solid, permanent marker carrying commemorative function. Cragg plays with the slow-time contemplative mode of the sculptural encounter that is expected through this traditional commemorative logic, and challenges the viewer with sculptures which are themselves highly evocative of change, flux and transformation. It is the 'in between' states and stages, and hybrid forms in the process of becoming, that preoccupy him most, as <u>Early Forms</u> and <u>Rational Beings</u> reveal. He uses the solid, obdurate materiality of sculpture, but uses it to articulate complicated spatial–temporal movements and to create works that defy any monolithic morbidity. Visitors to these large, outdoor sculptures are caught by surprise and kept looking, thinking and on their toes, perhaps as he himself was when making them. This is sculpture at the service of the mind, but also, importantly, sculpture at the service of life rather than death. Sculptures for dancing, not for dying. 'Never at Rest', as opposed to 'Rest in Peace', you might say, since Cragg's sculptures seem to offer themselves up as anti-funerary monuments: positive and dynamic commemorations of life and thought, designed to facilitate regeneration, rethinking and other ways of actively looking at and learning about things, of being alive.[5] Cragg's sculptures, to use that now famous quotation, can be read as 'thinking models to help you get through the world'.[6]

All this, in turn, is directly reflected in the duration and circumstances of sculpture-making: the inevitable disconnect between the time it takes to arrive at an idea, and the time it takes to carry it out. A sculptor can craft a form in clay in his or her hand, but a large-scale bronze, steel, wood fibre or fibreglass version may be realised only years later. The speed of change is thus simultaneously both slow and fast in Cragg's work, and in <u>Early Forms</u> and <u>Rational Beings</u> in particular. Indeed the speed of change and development, in turn, becomes part of what they are about, embedded and embodied in the works themselves. (The group title <u>Early Forms</u> itself denotes the beginning of a renewed, time-conscious oeuvre.) Change happens imperceptibly: both in a flash, in a millisecond, and gradually, over years. Since for Cragg, 'sculpture is Darwinian', this is both biological and artistic: resonant of the development of early animal and plant life, as it is of the development of an artist's work and oeuvre.[7] The finished sculptures can therefore, in a sense, be read as concrete commemorations of fugitive and changing states of mind, flash moments of artistic transition, as well as the slow course of process and development.

They are made in remembrance of these earlier and distant fleeting moments—visual approximations of germinative conceptions, which are then conducted and developed through the more gradual processes of the studio and foundry. For sculpture, as the photographs in this catalogue demonstrate only too well, is an art of patience, reflection, collaboration and teamwork, as well as of inspiration and individual artistic endeavour. As Cragg has said: 'Sculpture making profits enormously from experience… it is an empirical art.'[8]

<u>Early Forms</u> and <u>Rational Beings</u> are important and continuing groups of work that together have occupied Cragg for the last ten years or so. Though the former group

pre-dates the latter, he and his assistants have worked on them in tandem in the last few years, so both groups overlap and share the same real time and imaginative space. Early Forms show the gradual stretching and twisting evolution of an image-form in space, on the horizontal. The possibilities are endless, and as Cragg puts it, Early Forms has become a 'very generative and self-generating' group of works, with one version leading into another. [9/] Many start with vessels and bottles—forms of enclosure and containment that then have their enveloping skins folded open, turned inside out and stretched, revealing their inner spaces and volumes and their imagined, layered and lipped lives. A bottle will become a fantastic, multi-skinned shell that has been twisted into a totally new and startling configuration. In a sense, these hybrid Early Forms play out Cragg's meditation on the relationship between sculpture and design. A vessel is the starting point here in the search for new forms, new languages and new species. Early Forms thus mind the gaps between forms: showing what the intermediate possibilities of things might look like, and stretching them out with an eye-catching combination of organic and geometric shape. Looking both soft and hard, smooth and sharp-edged, Early Forms stand as commemorations of slow and fast change, of gradual and instant morphosis. They have the stubborn, fossil-like presence of earlier bronze works, such as Shell (1988) and Trilobites (1989), but their overall forms have now been hollowed out, twisted and accelerated. Though they seem to promise scientific explanation, they have come about through the direct, intuitive and experimental operations of the hand and imagination, not through the pre-formatted, two-dimensional possibilities of computer graphics. In keeping with this they also have an imaginary, artistic look—at once resonant of Henry Moore's post-war bronze reclining figures and of Umberto Boccioni's Development of a Bottle in Space (1913). Early Forms seem caught between these references, suspended in time between ancient and modern, between atavism and futurism, between prehistory and prototype, between the biological and the technological.

As with Meteorite, the directional play and energy of Early Forms is crucial. This group is developed on the horizontal, 'along a relatively simple bilaterally curved axis', with works that unravel their meanings back and forth, from left to right and back again. [10/] This gives them a palindromic movement, and a legibility 'on the loop', that takes the viewer's eye spinning on a roller-coaster ride around the sculptures. [11/] Sinbad, on display at Goodwood, is a prime example of this. Like a huge radiator, or a marine machine part that would not look out of place on the docks or at a shipyard, Sinbad has a glowing, golden patina that both evokes 'thermal heat' and defies its weightiness. Its intestinal machine-gut (which might recall the twisting drain pipes of Cragg's St George and the Dragon of 1984) carries the helter-skelter energy around the work, capturing our curiosity and desire.

Unlike Early Forms, Rational Beings play out their possibilities on the vertical, rather than the horizontal plane. And unlike Meteorite, which evoked an accelerated downwards movement, Rational Beings rise positively up into the air—gracefully defying gravity, gravitas and the grave, as Cragg would say, rolling etymological associations off his tongue and kicking ideas around in his head. Moreover, this 'family group' has in profile an anthropomorphic aspect that suggests the rotational and vertical development of psychological and physical states in transition. The anthropomorphic aspect is directly reflected in the titles that Cragg has used for them. Point of View and Bent of Mind are displayed here, from a larger group that also includes One Way or Another (2000) and In Two Minds, Line of Thought, Cast Glances and Changing Minds (all of 2002). Bent of Mind has connotations of a psychological state—a sculpture in two minds, caught between doubt and certainty. Point of View is a column of frenzied profiles, sharing the same integrated, material unit but looking, Janus-faced, both ways. It has a totemic quality, evocative of family trees and of ancestral and future lineage, which (like I'm Alive) brings us as viewers into its play through its shiny, reflective surface.

Relatives, another work in the Rational Beings group on display, makes these familial interconnections more explicit, more genetic, even: it is a bronze sculpture that pulls profiles in three dimensions, and across three axes, within a single over life-size, imaginary portrait bust. This speedy combinatory profiling takes further the strategies first witnessed in earlier works, such as Loco (1988), Untitled (1988) and In Camera (1993). Here Cragg has blended self-portraiture within large-scale wood and steel appropriations of Renato Giuseppe Bertelli's Continuous Profile—Head of Mussolini (1933). 'Loco' is Spanish for 'crazy', which gives these spinning heads a frenzied 'face value' that is later extended as 'family values' in Relatives. If Early Forms look along and back, stretching still-life into futuristic, primal form, then Rational Beings look up and forward, spinning portraiture into imaginary futures and pasts.

But if, in a sense, these sculptures of Cragg's are 'crazy', why then are they called Rational Beings? His own account of how they came about is useful in this respect. He writes: 'These sculptures are made by taking the contours of a gestural drawing and then filling them up or "fleshing them out" into the third dimension using circles of polystyrene which are then stuck together.'[13] Previously (in connection with works such as Wirbelsäule, for example), Cragg used drawing as a way of articulating the dynamic currents that might circulate a single free-standing sculpture — energising its immediate spatial environment, intellectually ventilating the work and highlighting the speed of the sculptural encounter at stake for the artist.[14] Now, such lively doodles have become the bases or templates for sculpture itself. For Cragg, the 'rationality' of this group comes from a number of aspects: from their being based on calculated drawings, from their ellipses and axes being carefully planned, and from the fact that they are constructed, piece by piece, from measured sections. Their 'rationality' is also, in part, indebted to their relationship to Cragg's earlier stacked works, such as Circles (1985), Pegs (1986) and Minsters (1987). These were assembled rather than constructed, by stacking one circular unit on top of another. 'Gravity was the glue' here, and the sculptures in a sense 'made themselves', as Cragg has said.[15] Though Rational Beings belong to this tradition, they are stuck and staked using an armature, the slim metal spine that fixes their swivelling dance to the spot.

These earlier works and the recent Rational Beings also reveal Cragg's constant fascination with things that have geologies: layers, strata, sediments and levels of deposit built up (and eroded) over time. Rational Beings have such a character— their height is also their 'depth' and their 'age'—but their settled stillness is immediately upset by the wobbling, spinning and off-kilter vertical forms and outlines of the sculptures themselves. Oval sections, or ellipses, have been staggered, shunted, one on top of another, and then sliced at an angle and smoothed away into amorphous, biomorphic sculptures. In the finished stone and kerto (reconstituted wooden) versions such streamlined strata can be easily seen. In works like Bent of Mind, however, this secret history is hidden behind a blind, and blinding, bronze skin.

Considering these hidden, horizontal layers might lead us to think of the natural world, and of trees in particular— of their outer bark and their inner rings that both reveal and conceal their age. Such associations are, of course, particularly pressing in the present environment, in the landscaped setting of Goodwood Sculpture Park. Surrounded by trees and plants that are always moving and always growing, Cragg's 'signs of life' have an extraordinary presence. Walking through the woods, we chance upon a perforated 'foreign body' that takes our breath away and then, through a clearing in the trees, we catch a glimpse of a strange, dark billowing object, rising up from the grass. Further on, where once there was only undergrowth, there is now a huge, white, chalk-pit crater. Coming out of the woods and drawing nearer, we stop in our tracks and see that somehow, at some time and from somewhere, a huge sculpture has landed in it.

9/
Ibid., Tape 28/33.
10/
Tony Cragg, 'To Viersen Sculpture', in Tony Cragg: Signs of Life, 2003, p. 459.
11/
See, for example, an Early Form, now in the collection of the Scottish National Gallery of Modern Art, called Kolbeblok.
12/
Tony Cragg interview, NLSC, 2004, Tape 27/33.
13/
Tony Cragg, 'To Viersen Sculpture', in Tony Cragg: Signs of Life, 2003, p. 458.
14/
See Anthony Cragg, Wirbelsäule, Stadtische Galerie im Park, Viersen, October–November 1996.
15/
Tony Cragg interview, NLSC, 2004, Tape 20/33.

TONY CRAGG— OUTDOOR SCULPTURES

BY JANE DUNCAN, ART & ARCHITECTURE JOURNAL

Discovering a contextual and symbolic relationship between artist and site that reaches beyond the ephemeral can be challenging; but such a partnership has been proposed at Goodwood. The recent reclamation, regeneration and landscaping of the chalk pit has produced a new 1.6 hectare extension to the woodland sculpture park and a site for solo artists exhibitions. It has launched with a group of thirteen outdoor sculptures by Tony Cragg creating the largest display of his work seen in Britain, with some pieces specially produced for the exhibition.

On the surface of it, Cragg's work and the chalk pit would appear unlikely bedfellows. But here lies the paradox: Through an almost phoenix like process of de-construction and re-construction, both have regenerated into bold, unique and homogeneous forms.

Currently celebrating its 10th anniversary, the Cass Sculpture Foundation was established by Wilfred and Jeannette Cass, with the principal objective being to advance the public enjoyment and appreciation of twenty-first century British sculpture, and also to support the developing careers of new and established artists. By contributing to the cost of creating new works, the Foundation allows artists the often-rare opportunity to work on a large scale, sometimes for the first time. In 2006, a 500m² education, archive and research centre designed by Studio Downie Architects will be opened. The 6.5m high gallery space will show indoor work and sculptures at various stages of the design process to complement the constantly changing display of large-scale sculpture outside. It will incorporate a lecture and conference facility for 200 people and the archive and library will house an extensive collection of aritsts' drawings, maquettes, videos and other resources that the Foundation has acquired over the years.

Tony Cragg was born in Liverpool in 1949. He studied at Gloucestershire College of Art and Design, Cheltenham, and the Royal College of Art, London, but for most of his life has lived and worked in Germany. He came to international prominence in the 1980s and has become one of the most widely exhibited artists of his generation.

Before attending art college Cragg worked as a laboratory technician at the Natural Rubber Producers Research Association (1966–68). It is perhaps here that his exploration of materials led to conceiving ideas for some of his most recognised works. Exploring surface and texture by creating works made from cast materials such as glass, plaster, iron, bronze, aluminium and stone. Surprisingly these pieces often attracted less attention than those made from recycled materials. In the early 1970s many of his works were made from found materials, demonstrating his continued interest in surface quality and the juxtaposition of shapes.

Cragg's early retrospective at the Hayward Gallery in 1987, was followed in 1988 by winning the Turner Prize and representing Britain at the Venice Biennale. These important milestones continued into the 1990s with significant exhibitions held at the Henry Moore Sculpture Studio in Halifax and a second show at the Whitechapel Gallery in 1997. In 1994 he was elected Royal Academician, and in 1999 an exhibition in the forecourt of Burlington House highlighted his new bronze sculptures. Following a solo exhibition at the Tate Liverpool in 2000, five monumental sculptures were sited on the terrace of Somerset House, London in Autumn 2001.

Despite this recognition, his work is often unfamiliar to audiences in Britain and he has rarely been offered public commissions. The exhibition at Goodwood, however, looks set to change public perception of his work. Approaching the site for the first time there is an almost humoristic irony to the setting; a bright green tongue of perfectly manicured grass, pours out from a distant corner of the mouth of the chalk pit. The contrasting white embankment rises and curves upwards to reveal a flat-topped grass plateau. At the centre sits Cragg's bronze sculpture Tongue in Cheek, a striking copper coloured perforated bronze hollow of intrigue, which commands the upper ridge. Declination, like all of Cragg's work in this

1/
*Tony Cragg quoted from A New
Thing Breathing, Tate Liverpool.*
2/
*Jocks, Heinz-Norbert, Tony Cragg:
Dieses Kleinzeug wirkt dannwie
ein Augenfang, Vergleichbar den
Warzen auf der Haut, Kunstforum
International, Vol.122, 193,
pp. 354–75.*
3/
*Tony Cragg quoted from A New
Thing Breathing, Tate Liverpool,
2000.*
4/
Ibid.

*Article first published in June 2005
by Art & Architecture Journal.*

exhibition, escapes categorisation, in spite of its bold colour and form and the sensual shapes within it, which invite an almost contemplative quality.

Observing Cragg's work in this uniquely landscaped context is an emphatic experience. It goes beyond language. Like the natural world surrounding the pieces, the work breathes, yet possesses an impenetrable delight, which exceeds any system, which might try to contain it.

'I have developed a particular belief in sculpture' says Cragg, 'It leads us to make things we had never envisaged, allowing us to experience emotions and ideas we may not have had by any other method.' [1]

But even with this inherent spiritual link, his work is still bound by a strong physical presence and profound sense of aesthetic, which continues to be reflected in his broad choice of materials. Always forward thinking, Cragg believes: 'In the future it will become more and more important to make visible this huge amount of imperceptible information, which is related to the perceptible. If we look at the world of molecules, energy waves or the like, it will become necessary to find a language to describe the invisible, inaudible, the unsmellable or the untouchable. That could be a function of sculpture.' [2]

It is not surprising therefore that Cragg's interest in transcending inanimate materiality is implied through exploring the rich language and subtle qualities of shape, colour and surface texture. Bent of Mind, a bronze weighing 5.5 tonnes, appears to exude features similar to that of the human face, whilst its neighbouring Here Today Gone Tomorrow seems to be engaged in a layer of subliminal dialogue. If these pieces are characteristic of Cragg's most recent work in bronze and stone, then the dynamics of I'm Alive illuminates a process of material exploration leaping both visually and symbolically into the future. In this piece, the evolutionary like form arches towards an invisible realm, whilst its stainless steel skin reflects the light and colours of the immediate environment.

At the core of Cragg's work is the use of subtle markers to define and explore regeneration. Whether through transformation via the materials he uses to create his work, or re-thinking ways to identify his intuitive philosophies, he is constantly involved in a process. Unlike many artists he has never become entrenched in a dialogue of repetitive style. His work is forever evolving, and the exhibition at Goodwood provides an excellent opportunity to explore examples from this journey. Bulb, a 15 tonnes stone sculpture, created by Cragg in 2000, and Formulations (Stance) a bronze, also from this period, offer interesting comparatives with other more recent work in these mediums. Free interpretation is one of the joys of viewing public art and comments from the artist often reveal the true motivations behind the work: 'I am continuing to search for knowledge, while I dig in unexpected corners of our world.' [3]

It is impossible to completely define Cragg's work, but there is an emphatic physicality in his sculptures that inform, declare and surprise all at the same time. His themes demonstrate not only a process of contrast in regeneration, but also indicate a conviction of self-belief, an almost evolutionary framework that interconnects physical representation and philosophy. Though Cragg is no stranger to devising compelling ways of making us see, his new work provides unexpected insights that arise purely from experiencing these sculptures in such a unique and natural setting. In tandem with its urban forerunner, the Fourth Plinth in Trafalgar Square; The chalk pit at Goodwood looks set to become another iconic setting for public art.

'So the sculptures remain what they should be, not rational demonstrations, but fictional entities where decisions are made entirely on an aesthetic basis.' [4]

TONY CRAGG BIOGRAPHY 1949–

Born in Liverpool, England	1949
Lab Technician at the National Rubber Producers Research Association	1966–1968
Gloucestershire College of Art, Cheltenham	1969–1970
Wimbledon School of Art	1970–1973
Royal College of Art	1973–1977
Professor L'Ecole des Beaux Arts de Metz	1976
Moved to Wuppertal	1977
Beginning of exhibitions	1977
Teaching at the Kunstakademie, Düsseldorf	1978–1988
First solo exhibition at the Lisson Gallery, London	1979
British representative at the 43rd Venice Biennale	1988
Turner Prize	1988
Professorship at the Kunstakademie, Düsseldorf	1988–2001
Co-director at the Kunstakademie Düsseldorf	1989–2001
Von-der-Heydt-Prize	1989
Chevalier des Arts et des Lettres	1992
Royal Academician	1994
Honorary Professorship, Budapest	1996
Professorship at the Universität der Künste (UdK), Berlin	2001
Shakespeare Prize	2001
Honorary degree award of Doctor of the University of Surrey	2001
Honorary fellowship John Moores University, Liverpool	2001
Akademie der Künste, Berlin	2001
CBE	2002
Piepenbrock Preis für Skulptur	2002
Lives and works in Wuppertal, Germany	2005–

TONY
CRAGG
SCULPTURE
INFORMATION

Declination	2005	Bronze	2.4 x 2.3 x 3.6m	2.7 tonnes
Bent of Mind	2005	Bronze	4.7 x 2.7 x 2.7m	5.5 tonnes
I'm Alive	2005	Stainless Steel	2.5 x 3.9 x 3.6m	4 tonnes
Relatives	2004	Bronze	0.7 x 0.7 x 0.6m	0.6 tonnes
On a Roll	2004	Bronze	0.8 x 1.5 x 0.9m	0.2 tonnes
Point of View	2004	Stainless Steel	3 x 0.8 x 0.7m	0.3 tonnes
Sinbad	2003	Bronze	1.6 x 3.1 x 1.7m	2.7 tonnes
Here Today Gone Tomorrow	2002	Stone	4.5 x 1.2 x 1.2m	14 tonnes
Cast Glances	2002	Bronze	2.4 x 1.9 x 1.6m	1 tonne
Tongue in Cheek	2002	Bronze	1.3 x 1.7 x 2.3m	0.8 tonnes
Ferryman	2001	Bronze	3.9 x 1.9 x 1.2m	1.3 tonnes
Formulations (Stance)	2000	Bronze	2.2 x 1 x 1m	0.6 tonnes
Bulb	2000	Stone	3.3 x 1.8 x 1.8m	15 tonnes

TONY CRAGG EXHIBITIONS 1979–

Lisson Gallery, London	1979	
Lützowstr. Situation, Berlin	1979	
Künstlerhaus Weidenallee, Hamburg	1979	
Galerie Konrad Fischer, Düsseldorf	1979	
Arnolfini Gallery, Bristol	1980	
Konrad Fischer, Düsseldorf	1980	
Lisson Gallery, London	1980	
Galerie Chantal Crousel, Paris	1980	
Lützowstr. Situation, Büro Berlin, Berlin	1980	
Lucio Amelio, Naples	1980	
Franco Toselli, Mailand	1980	
Saman Gallery, Genua	1980	
Büro Berlin, Berlin	1980	
Schellmann & Klüser, München	1981	
Musée d'Art et d'Industrie, St. Etienne	1981	23/01–08/03
Whitechapel Art Gallery, London	1981	
Nouveau Musée, Lyon	1981	
Front Room, London	1981	
Von der Heydt Museum, Wuppertal	1981	
Vacuum, Düsseldorf	1981	
Badischer Kunstverein, Karlsruhe	1982	12/01–28/02
Kanransha Gallery, Tokyo	1982	
Nisshin Gallery, Tokyo	1982	
Marian Goodman Gallery, New York	1982	
Le Nouveau Musée (NDLR), Lyon	1982	
Büro Berlin, Berlin	1982	
Galerie Chantal Crousel, Paris	1982	
Schellmann & Klüser, München	1982	
Lisson Gallery, London	1982	
Galerie Konrad Fischer, Düsseldorf	1982	
Rijksmuseum Kröller-Müller, Otterloo	1982	
Fifth Triennale India, New Delhi	1982	
Lucio Amelio, Naples	1983	
Marian Goodman Gallery, New York	1983	
Kunsthalle Bern	1983	30/04–05/06
Art & Project, Amsterdam	1983	
Galeria Thomas Cohn, Rio de Janeiro	1983	
Galerie Buchmann, St Gallen	1983	
Franco Toselli, Mailand	1983	
Yarlow & Salzmann, Toronto	1984	
De Vleeshal, Middelburg, Holland	1984	13/01
Louisiana Museum of Modern Art, Humlebaek, Denmark	1984	
Schellmann & Klüser, München	1984	
Marian Goodman, New York	1984	
Kanransha Gallery, Tokyo	1984	
Crousel-Hussenot, Paris	1984	
Kölnischer Kunstverein, Köln	1984	
Galleria Tucci Russo, Turin	1984	
Kunsthalle Waaghaus, Winterthur	1985	
Staatsgalerie Moderner Kunst, München	1985	
Donald Young Gallery, Chicago	1985	
Lisson Gallery, London	1985	
Art & Project, Amsterdam	1985	
Palais des Beaux-Arts, Brüssel	1985	20/06–28/07
ARC, Musée d'Art Moderne de la Ville de Paris, Paris	1985	
Galerie Bernd Klüser, München	1985	
Kestner-Gesellschaft, Hannover	1985	20/12–09/02
Galerie Buchmann, Basel	1986	
Joost Declercq, Ghent	1986	
The Brooklyn Museum, Brooklyn	1986	
Marian Goodman Gallery, New York	1986	

University Art Museum, University of California, Berkeley	1986	
'Raliegh' commissioned by the Tate Gallery, London	1986	
Geward, Ghent	1986	
Pierre Huber, Genf	1986	
Galerie Konrad Fischer, Düsseldorf	1986	
Hayward Gallery, London	1987	05/03–07/06
Corner House, Manchester	1987	
Galleria Tucci Russo, Turin	1987	
Kanransha Gallery, Tokyo	1987	
Marian Goodman Gallery, New York	1987	
Venice Biennale	1988	26/06–25/09
Galerie Marga Paz, Madrid	1988	
Galerie Klüser, München	1988	
Galerie Buchmann, Basel	1988	
Galerie Crousel-Robelin, Paris	1988	
Foksal Gallery, Warsaw	1988	
Lisson Gallery, London	1988	
Silo, Val de Valse	1988	18/06–30/08
Marian Goodman Gallery, New York	1989	
Galerie Konrad Fischer, Düsseldorf	1989	
Kanransha Gallery, Tokyo	1989	
'Ordovician Pore' commissioned by the Walker Art Center	1989	
Kunstsammlung Nordrhein-Westfalen, Düsseldorf	1989	18/11/1989–07/01/1999
Tate Gallery, London	1989	26/04–25/06
Galeria Thomas Cohn, Rio	1989	
Stedelijk Van Abbemuseum, Eindhoven	1989	05
Crown Point Press, San Francisco	1990	
Galerie Buchmann, Basel	1990	
'Early Forms' commissioned by the Von der Heydt Museum, Wuppertal	1990	
'Early Forms' commissioned by the Houston Museum of Fine Arts	1990	
Galleria Tucci Russo, Turin	1990	
Kanransha Gallery, Tokyo	1990	
Newport Harbor Art Museum, Newport Beach	1990	14/10–30/12
Galerie Klüser, München	1990	
Galerie Konrad Fischer, Düsseldorf	1990	
Valentina Moncada, Rom	1990	30/11/1990–15/01/1991
Wiener Secession, Wien	1991	02/10–03/11
Lisson Gallery, London	1991	
Marian Goodman, New York	1991	
Power Plant, Toronto	1991	06/09–27/10
Galerie Crousel-Robelin, Paris	1991	
Werkstatt Kollerschlag, Kollerschlag	1991	
Van Abbemuseum, Eindhoven	1991	
Galerie Klüser, München	1991	
The Contemporary Arts Museum, Houston	1991	16/11/1991–09/02/1992
Art & Project, Niederlande	1991	
The Corcoran Gallery of Art, Washington DC	1991	01/02–31/03
IVAM Valencia	1992	21/01–22/03
Galerie Buchmann, Basel	1992	
Musée departemental d'art contemporain, Rochechouart	1992	
Centre d'art Contemporain, Kerguéhennec	1992	04/07–01/11
Group of four sculptures, commissioned by the Landeszentralbank, Düsseldorf	1992	
Tramway, Glasgow	1992	25/07–06/09
CCA, Glasgow	1992	
Isy Brachot, Brüssel	1992	06/02–28/03
Galeria Thomas Cohn, Sao Paulo	1992	
Galleria Tucci Russo, Turin	1992	
Lisson Gallery, London	1992	
Mala Galerija, Moderna Galerija , Ljubljana	1992	18/12/1992–10/01/1993
'Archimedes Screw', commissioned by the town of 's-Hertogenbosch	1993	03
Knoll Galéria, Budapest	1993	
Studio Barnabo, Venice	1993	
Ganserhaus, Wasserburg/Inn	1993	
Galerie Hachmeister, Münster	1993	
Galerie Buchmann, Basel	1993	
Marian Goodman Gallery, New York	1994	
Musée des Beaux-Arts, Nantes	1994	
Effe Arte, Lecco	1994	

Stadtgalerie, Saarbrücken	1994	
'Daily Bread', commissioned by Neustadt, Wien	1994	
Galérie Crousel-Robelin, Paris	1994	
Galleria Civica d'Arte Contemporanea, Trento	1994	28/05–10/07
Stadtgalerie Saarbrücken	1994	
Gesellschaft für Gegenwartskunst, Augsburg	1994	17/11–30/12
Galerie Bernd Klüser, München	1994	
Kunstverein, St Gallen	1994	
Kunst auf der Zugspitze, Garmisch-Partenkirchen	1995	
Galerie Buchmann, Basel	1995	
OTTO, Bologna	1995	
Tucci Russo Studio per l'Arte Contemporanea,		
Torre Pellice (Torino)	1995	
Galerie Buchmann, Basel	1995	
Kunsthaus Bruno, Dum umení mesta Brna	1995	26/06–13/08
Nationalgalerie Prag, Valdsteinská		
jízdarna v Praze, Prag	1995	20/06–23/07
Galerie Hachmeister, Münster	1995	
Museo Nacional Centro de Arte Reina Sofia, Madrid	1995	
Deweer Art Gallery, Otegem	1995	04/02–05/03
Nova Sin, Prag	1995	
Henry Moore Foundation, Halifax	1996	
Galerie Karsten Greve, Paris	1996	
Müczanok Kunsthalle Budapest	1996	
Middelheim Sculpture Park, Antwerpen	1996	08/09–24/11
Galerie im Park, Viersen	1996	
'Wirbelsäule', commissioned by Stadt Viersen	1996	10
'Zufuhr', commissioned by Sparkasse Wuppertal	1996	
'Wave Forms', commissioned by the Battery Park Authority	1996	
Galerie Mauroner, Salzburg	1996	
'World Events', Commissioned by the IOC	1996	
Freundeskreis Wilhelmshöhe e.V., Ettlingen	1996	
Buchmann Galerie, Köln	1996	
Lehmbruck Museum, Duisburg	1996	
Carin Delcourt van Krimpen, Amsterdam	1996	
MNAM, Centre Georges Pompidou, Paris	1996	24/01–15/04
Atelier des Enfants, Centre Georges Pompidou, Paris	1996	
Galerie Karsten Greve, Milano	1996	
Whitechapel Art Gallery, London	1997	10/01–09/03
Lisson Gallery, London	1997	10/01–09/03
Nationalgalerie Skopje	1997	20/02–14/03
Nationalgalerie Sofia	1997	
Toyota Municipal Museum of Art, Toyota	1997	25/03–22/06
Nationalgalerie Bratislava	1997	17/04–01/06
Biennale Venedig, Venedig	1997	
Bawag Fondation, Wien	1997	25/06–11/10
Art Gallery of New South Wales, Sydney	1997	
National Museum of Contemporary Art Korea, Seoul	1997	02/08–03/09
Queensland Art Gallery, Brisbane	1997	
Galerie Meyer-Ellinger, Frankfurt	1997	
Nationalgalerie, Ujazdowskie Castle, Warschau	1997	
BEL, Banque Européen, Luxemburg	1997	
MACBA, Barcelona	1997	
Bunkier Sztuki, Krakow	1997	
Galerie Bernd Klüser, München	1997	
Sennestadt GmbH, Bielefeld	1997	
Kenji Taki Gallery, Nagoya	1998	
Wellington City Gallery, Wellington	1998	
Galerie Karsten Greve, Paris	1998	
The Contemporary Art Center of Vilnius, Vilnius	1998	
Marian Goodman Gallery, New York	1998	
The Association of Latvian Art Museums, Riga	1998	
Ulmer Museum, Ulm	1998	26/04–21/06
Galerie Seitz-von Werder, Berlin	1998	
Tallin Art Hall, Tallin	1998	
Commune di Siena, Siena	1998	19/06–04/10
Lenbachhaus, München	1998	15/07–20/09
Deweer Art Gallery, Otegem	1998	31/10–20/12
Lisson Gallery, London	1998	
Sara Hildenin Taidemuseo, Tampere	1999	30/01–09/05
Galerie Chantal Crousel, Paris	1999	03
Galerie Konrad Fischer, Düsseldorf	1999	

Studio per l'arte Contemporanea Tucci		
Russo, Torre Pellice (Torino)	1999	09
Barmenia Versicherungen, Wuppertal	1999	
Von-der-Heydt-Museum Wuppertal, 'Atelier: Wuppertal'	1999	30/05–18/07
Museum Dhondt-Dhaenens, Deurle	1999	
Galleri Stefan Andersson, Sweden	1999	
Royal Academy Summer Exhibition, London	1999	
Galeria André Viana, Porto	1999	11/12
Kenji Taki Gallery, Nagoya/Tokyo	1999	
Museum Het Kruithuis, s-Hertogenbosch	1999	
Buchmann Galerie, Köln	1999	
Galerie der Stadt Stuttgart	1999	10/12–27/02
Tate Gallery, Liverpool	2000	17/03–04/06
Glyndebourne, England	2000	
Kunstverein Springhornhof, Neuenkirchen	2000	27/05–27/08
I8 Galleri, Reykjavik, Iceland	2000	
Holderbank, Holderbank, Schweiz, 'Sculptures in the Shade'	2000	06–08
Butler Gallery, Kilkenny	2000	12/10–26/11
Bernd Klüser Galerie, München,		
Münchener Kunstwochendende Open Art	2000	09
Muhka, Antwerpen	2000	07/10–21/01
Model Arts Centr, Sligo	2000	12/10–26/11
Marian Goodman Gallery, New York	2000	
Karsten Greve, Paris	2000	
Bernier/Eliades, Athen	2001	
Galerie Seitz, Berlin	2001	10/03–05/05
Glynn Vivian Art Gallery, Swansea	2001	04–06
Galerie Meyer-Ellinger, Frankfurt	2001	
Malmö Konsthall, Malmö, Sweden	2001	28/04–19/08
Thomas Cohn Galeria, Sao Paulo, Brazil	2001	10/05–09/06
Studio per l'arte Contemporanea		
Tucci Russo, Torre Pellice (Torino)	2001	
Stadtsparkasse Wuppertal, Wuppertal	2001	06
Kunstsammlungen Chemnitz, Chemnitz	2001	24/06–02/09
Galeria Academia, Salzburg	2001	19/07–30/09
Somerset House, London	2001	
Lisson Gallery, London	2001	
Galleri Stefan Andersson, Umea, Sweden	2001	
Deweer Art Gallery, Otegem	2002	10/03–28/04
Galerie Epikur, Wuppertal	2002	13/04–29/06
Buchmann Galerie, Köln	2002	
Dunkers Kulturhus, Helsingborg	2002	
Lippische Gesellschaft für Kunst, Detmold	2002	12/05–23/07
Bethmann Bank, Frankfurt	2002	
Galeria Charles Taché, Barcelona	2002	11–12
Galerie Crousel, Paris	2003	17/01
Bibliothèque Nationale Francaise, Paris	2003	03/08
Galerie Seitz und Partner, Berlin	2003	
Kunst-und Ausstellungshalle der		
Bundesrepublik Deutschland, Bonn	2003	23/05–05/10
CAC Málaga, Malaga	2003	31/05
MACRO Museum of Contemporary Art, Rome	2003	07/07–07/09
Galerie Bernd Klüser, München,		
Tony Cragg 'Recent Sculptures'	2003	11/09–08/11
Thomas Cohn Galeria, Sao Paulo	2003	10–11
Marian Goodman Gallery, New York	2003	04
Milliken Gallery, Stockholm	2004	01/04–22/05
Kenji Taki Gallery, Nagoya/Tokyo	2004	21/05–26/06
Buchmann Galerie, Köln	2004	
Hans Knoll Galerie, Wien	2004	05/06–30/06
Museu Serralves, Porto	2004	18/07–17/10
Galeria Carles Taché, Barcelona	2005	03/03–
Studio per l'Arte Contemporanea, Torre Pellice, Italy	2005	05
Gow Langsford Gallery, Auckland, New Zealand	2005	05
Cass Sculpture Foundation, Goodwood, England	2005	05
Galerie Thaddaeus Ropac, Paris	2005	05
The Central House of Artists, Moscow	2005	06

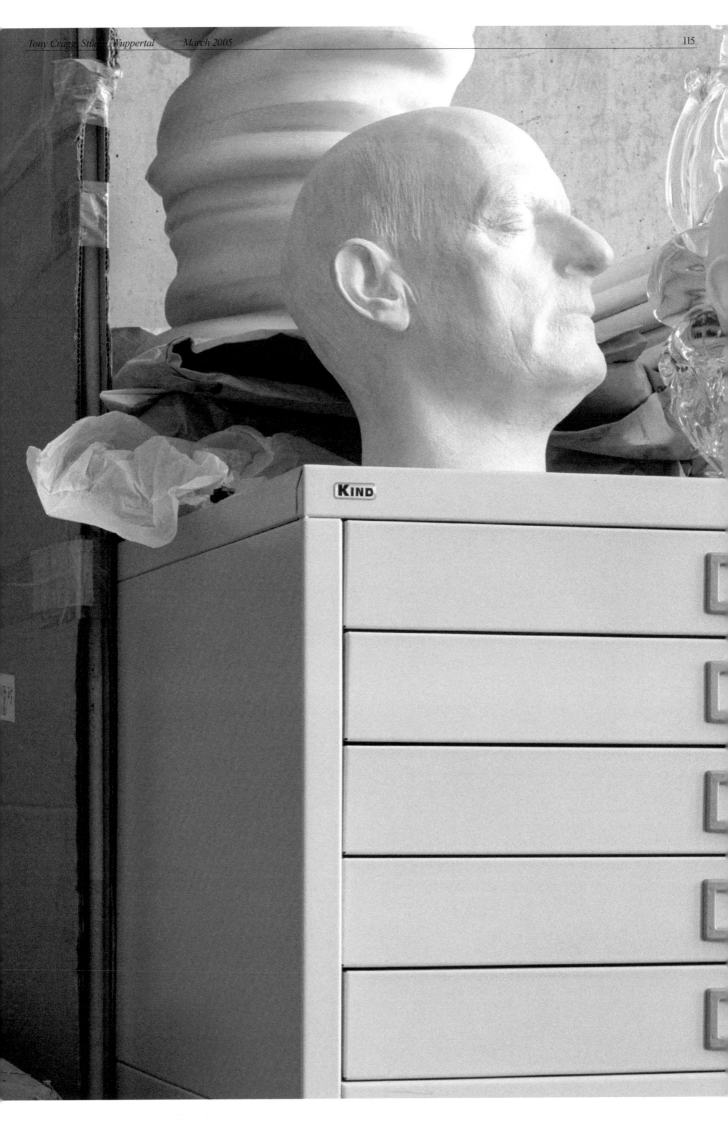

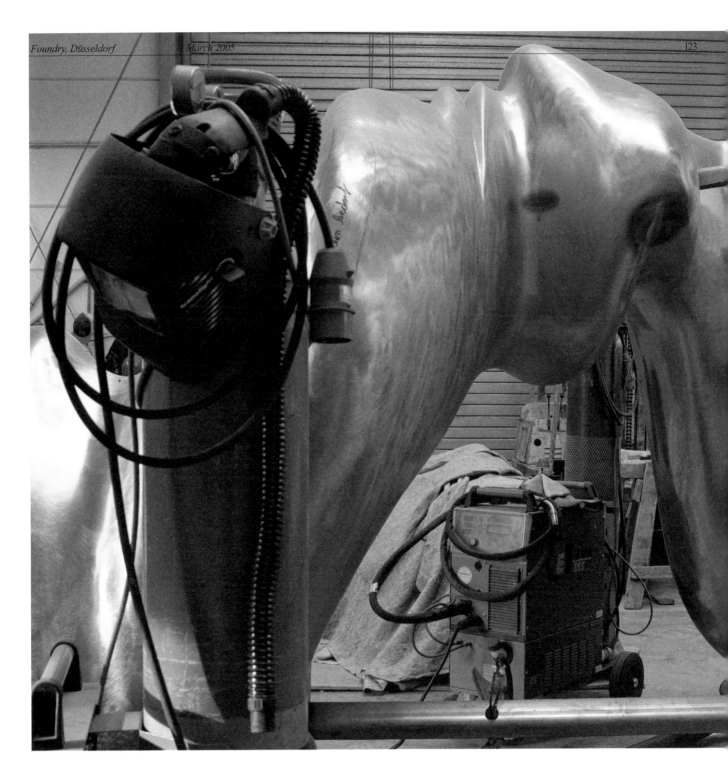

IT IS A VERY COMMON ARTISTIC METHOD,

TO USE TECHNIQUES IN WHICH ACCUMU- LATIONS OF PARTICLES ARE DEPLOYED.

THIS IS THE BASIC PRINCIPLE OF PAINTING AND DRAWING,

AND HAS BEEN USED IN SCULPTURE IN MANY WORKS.

I HAVE MADE SEVERAL WORKS WHICH HAVE USED THIS FORM,

AND I KNOW THAT THE COMPLICATED RELATIONSHIP BETWEEN THE MATERIAL,

OBJECT AND IMAGE,

PROVIDES SEEMINGLY ENDLESS POSSIBILITIES OF FORM AND MEANING.

WE HAVE GROWN UP FOR MILLIONS OF YEARS,

IN THE PRESENCE OF THE NATURAL WORLD AROUND US,

AND HAVE HAD TIME TO EVOLVE A RELATIONSHIP WITH THE OBJECTS IN IT.

BECAUSE OF THE WAY AND SPEED IN WHICH WE PRODUCE NEW MATERIALS,

AND OBJECTS,

WE DO NOT HAVE THE TIME TO DEVELOP A MEANINGFUL RELATIONSHIP WITH THESE MATERIALS.

TRYING TO GIVE THESE THINGS MORE MEANING,

MYTHOLOGY AND POETRY IS THE CLEAR PREDICATE OF ART IN THIS CENTURY.

A
ROUND
BALL,

A
BENT
BANANA,

A
FAT
MAN
AND
A
RUSHING
RIVER,

ARE
ALL
SEEN
IN
THE
LIGHT
OF
OUR
DAILY
EXPERIENCES
WITH
THEM.

WE
HAVE
AN
UNDER-
STANDING
OF
THEIR
FORMS
BASED
ON
THE
ROLE
THEY
PLAY
IN
OUR
LIVES.

THEREFORE,
IT
IS
DIFFICULT
TO
USE
A
SQUARE
BALL,

AND
A
SPHERICAL
RIVER
WOULD
CHALLENGE
ITS
DEFINITION
AS
MUCH
AS
A
FLAT
MAN
OR
A
GASEOUS
BANANA
WORLD.

I
AM
CONTINUING
TO
SEARCH
FOR
MORE
KNOWLEDGE,

WHILE
I
DIG
IN
UNEXPECTED
CORNERS
OF
OUR
WORLD.

IF
WE
LOOK
AT
THE
WORLD
OF
MOLECULES,

ENERGY
WAVES
OR
THE
LIKE,

IT
WILL
BECOME
NECESSARY
TO
FIND
A
LANGUAGE
TO
DESCRIBE
THE
INVISIBLE,

THE
INAUDIBLE,

THE
UNSMELLABLE
OR
THE
UNTOUCHABLE.

THAT
COULD
BE
A
FUNCTION
OF
SCULPTURE.

SCULPTURE, OF ALL THE OBJECTS AND THINGS THAT HUMAN BEINGS DEEM NECESSARY TO MAKE THEIR LIVES MORE LIVEABLE,

BELONGS FOR SEVERAL REASONS IN A RARE AND EXTRA-ORDINARY CLASS OF ITS OWN.

RARE, BECAUSE EVEN JUST LOOKED AT QUANT-ITATIVELY,

VERY FEW KILOGRAMS OF SCULPTURE ARE MADE ON AN AVERAGE DAY,

WHILE MANY BILLIONS OF TONS OF MATERIALS ARE MADE INTO OTHER MORE 'USEFUL' THINGS.

EXTRA-ORDINARY, BECAUSE ALTHOUGH SCULPTURE REMAINS FOR THE GREATER PART USELESS,

UNLIKE DESIGNED OBJECTS,

IT IS AN ATTEMPT TO MAKE DUMB MATERIAL EXPRESS HUMAN THOUGHTS AND EMOTIONS.

I
HAVE
DEVELOPED
A
PARTICULAR
BELIEF
IN
SCULPTURE
MAKING,

THAT
I
THINK
GIVES
IT
A
PRINCIPLE
AND
IMPORTANT
ROLE.

WHAT
FASCINATES
ME
IS
THE
WAY
IN
WHICH
WE
WORK
WITH
MATERIALS,

LIKE
PEN
AND
PAPER,

OR
A
PIECE
OF
CLAY,

OR
ANY
OTHER
MATERIAL
FOR
THAT
MATTER,

AND
WHILE
WE
ARE
WORKING
WITH
THIS
MATERIAL,

IT
SEEMS
TO
SUGGEST
THINGS
TO
US.

LEADING
US
TO
MAKE
THINGS
WE
HAD
NEVER
ENVISAGED,

AND
ALLOWING
US
TO
EXPERIENCE
EMOTIONS
AND
IDEAS
WE
MAY
NOT
HAVE
HAD
BY
ANY
OTHER
METHOD,

AND
DEFINITELY
WOULD
NOT
HAVE
HAD
BY
SITTING
IN
THE
CORNER
AND
CONCEPT-
UALISING.

THIS
HAPPENS
WHEN
PEOPLE
ARE
MAKING
SCULPTURE.

Tony Cragg, Studio, Wuppertal   *March 2005*

Published by Cass Sculpture Foundation
Copyright © 2005
ISBN 0-9357794-7-5

Edited by Mark Cass
Design by MadeThought
Photography by Leon Chew
Print by The Colourhouse

Registered Charity No. 1015088
Company No. 3920131

Cass Sculpture Foundation
Goodwood, West Sussex PO18 OQP
Phone +44 (0)1243 538 449
3+4 Percy Street, London W1T 1DF
Phone +44 (0)20 7637 0129
Email info@sculpture.org.uk
www.sculpture.org.uk

0 10596999

cass sculpture
foundation